"Captain of the C]

A tribute to Captain Eric "W

Background notes supporting the presentation of

**"Beardmore Built".
"HMS Argus 1914 to 1947, The World's
First Flat Top Aircraft Carrier"**

At

Rolls Royce Heritage Trust

Scottish Branch

Inchinnan, February 2017

By

Alan Morrison

Bucker Jungmann

Hanna Reitsch in the cockpit of the Focke Achgelis helicopter, with Ernst Udet giving instructions

Commanding Officer RNAS Lossiemouth
Buccaneer strike aircraft in the background

Nerton Publishing Ltd

Copyright: Nerton Publishing Limited 2017

Printed in Glasgow by Merchant City Print

ISBN: 978-0-9573443-6-5
First Published: February 2017. 2nd impression December 2017
Editor: Iain C. MacKay   **Graphics**: Nerton Publishing Ltd

Regular Navy Career 1940 to 1970

1/40-4/40 Flying Refresher Course (RNAS Sydenham)
5/40-8/40 Advanced Operational Flying Course (RAF Netheravon)
9/40-11/40 759(FT) Squadron (RNAS Yeovilton)
11/40-11/40 801(F) Squadron (RNAS Hatston, Orkney).
12/40-12/41 802(F) Squadron (RNAS Donibristle, HMS Audacity)
2/42-4/42 802(F) Squadron (RNAS Yeovilton)
5/42-7/42 768 (DLT) Squadron (RNAS Arbroath, HMS Argus)
8/42-9/42 897(F) Squadron (RNAS Stretton)
9/42-12/43 778(STU) Squadron (RNAS Arbroath, RNAS Crail)
12/43-1/44 Naval Test Squadron (A&AEE Boscombe Down)
1/44-8/49 Chief Naval Test Pilot, Royal Aircraft Establishment, Farnborough
8/49-11/49 School of Naval Air Warfare (RNAS St. Merryn)
11/49-7/51 802(F) Squadron (RNAS Culdrose, HMS Vengeance, HMS Indomitable)
9/51-11/52 Flight Test, US Naval Air Test Center, Patuxent River, MD
2/53-8/53 Ship's Officer, HMS Rocket (Londonderry)
8/53-8/53 Helicopter Refresher Course (RNAS Gosport)
8/53-10/53 SAR Helicopter Flight, HMS Illustrious
10/53-11/53 Jet Flying Refresher Course (RNAS Brawdy)
11/53-7/54 CO, 804(F) Squadron (RNAS Lossiemouth)
7/54-11/56 Commander (Air), RNAS Brawdy
11/56-5/57 Joint Services Staff College (Latimer)
5/57-6/57 Instrument Flying Course (RNAS Ford).
7/57-12/57 RAF Flying College Advanced Air Warfare Course (RAF Manby).
1/58-9/60 British Naval Air Mission to Germany (Kiel and Schleswig)
1/61-2/62 Deputy Director (Air), Gunnery Division, Ministry of Defence
2/62-9/64 Deputy Director, Naval Air Warfare Division, Ministry of Defence
9/64-10/64 Royal Naval Tactical School (Woolwich)
11/64-5/67 British Naval Attaché, Bonn, West Germany
8/67-9/67 Instrument Flying Course (RNAS Brawdy)
9/67-3/70 CO, RNAS Lossiemouth
3/70 Retired from active service in the Royal Navy

Some Notable Flying Events

1. World record number of Carrier Trap Deck Landings - 2,407.
2. World Record number of Catapult Launches (at sea and on land) - 2,721.
3. World Record number of aircraft basic types (not marks or models) flown as command pilot - 487.
4. First carrier deck landing of a British twin Jet Aircraft (Meteor), 8 June 1948.
5. World's first carrier deck landing of a jet aircraft (Vampire), 3 December 1945.
6. First deck landing of a tricycle aircraft (Airacobra) on a British carrier, 3 April 1944.
7. First carrier deck landing of a British high-performance twin- engine aircraft (Mosquito), 25 March 1944.
8. Last pilot of the Me163 Komet rocket fighter.

Me163 Komet

*Smashed Me163 skid
at RAF Wittering*

Eric M. Brown

During his 31-year career in the Royal Navy, Eric "Winkle" Brown flew a world-record 487 aircraft types and performed a record-shattering 2,407 carrier landings, which has never been equalled. In addition, he performed the world's first jet landing on an aircraft carrier. He was the world's foremost carrier and test pilot and during the Second World War he was posted to HMS Argus on the Firth of Clyde, Scotland as an instructor, which he did not enjoy. "Winkle" refers to his physical size.

Eric Melrose Brown was born in Leith, Scotland on the 21st January 1919. His parents were from the Borders and lived in Edinburgh. His father, Robert Brown, had been a balloon observer in the Royal Flying Corps during the Great War and at the time of the Armistice in 1918 had been trained as a pilot. Eric was educated in Edinburgh and won a scholarship to the Royal High School and excelled in sports. With the death of his mother, Eric's father returned to the Borders, Eric commuting daily to school. His father was also a member of the Auxiliary Air Force, flying Gloster Gauntlets. On many occasions the young Eric Brown would sit in the Gauntlet's cockpit, working the controls, whetting his flying appetite.

With an invitation from former German Great War pilots in 1936, his father took him to the Berlin Olympic Games. There he met the German aeronautical greats, including Ernst Udet and Hanna Reitsch. He also flew with Udet in a Bucker Jungmann aerobatic trainer. It was Udet who strapped him into the Jungmann at the airfield. Udet put on a full aerobatic routine for the young Eric and pushed the Jungmann to its limits. Whilst on the approach to land, Udet inverted the Jungmann at about fifty feet above the runway, rolling the aircraft upright, as he landed he yelled out "Hals und Beinbruch!" the German fighter pilot's exclamation. After the flight Udet told him that he should fly and learn German.

In 1937 he joined the University Air unit at Edinburgh and majored in foreign languages, principally German. With a view to entering the Foreign Service, he became a Civil Service Cadet, being sent to France and Germany, with six months in each country as part of his cadetship. In February 1938 he returned to Germany and called on Udet in Berlin. Udet took him to see Hannah Reitsch flying the Focke Achgelis helicopter in the Deutschlandhalle. He was in Germany when the Second World War broke out in September 1939, teaching at Salem International College on the banks of Lake Constance. One morning he was awakened by a loud knock at his door. As he opened the door, a woman interpreter loudly proclaimed, "Our countries are at war". He was escorted to the Swiss border and lost everything except his MG sports car. When he asked the Germans why he was being allowed to keep the car, he was promptly told, "We have no spares". Racing home, he was concerned that the war would end before he was able to join the action. He returned to Britain via Switzerland and the channel ports in France.

Eric Brown wanted to fly with the Royal Air Force, but this was going to take longer than he had anticipated, so he decided to offer his services to the Fleet Air Arm instead. He was sent to Gosport to learn naval routine and from there to Northern Ireland to train on Miles Magisters, having decided on fighters as his professional choice. This was June 1940, the "Dark Days" in Britain's war. From Belfast he went to Yeovilton, to train on Gloster Gladiators. His first encounter with the Luftwaffe was to intercept Heinkel bombers, but he lost the kill to anti-aircraft fire.

Brown's first naval posting was to 802 Squadron at Donibristle in Fife, but he was immediately sent to 810 squadron, Orkneys, to take part in a raid to Norway, flying Blackburn Skuas. The raid was against oil storage tanks at Bergen. With great excitement he returned to Donibristle to fly the new Grumman Martlet, later called "Wildcat". The Martlet was a high performance U.S. Navy fighter that had been bought by France and with the fall of France the order was taken over by the Royal Navy. On the 14th May he flew his Martlet to Croydon for modifications, but had to divert to Cranwell due to bad weather. There he saw Britain's first jet aircraft, the Gloster E28/39. After modification the Martlets were flown to Arbroath from Fife for deck landing training.

At this time in the war there was a great shortage of aircraft carriers for convoy protection. Convoys were being attacked by the Luftwaffe FW 200 Condor, which was also directing U boats to attack the convoys. Churchill had come up with a plan to convert merchantmen to auxiliary aircraft carriers, but there was a great shortage of merchant vessels. The conversion plan now centred on a captured German vessel, named "*Hannover*." Carrying a cargo of plywood, she had been intercepted by the cruiser *Dunedin* and towed to Jamaica. From there she was taken to Glasgow and her cargo of plywood recycled for the aircraft industry by H. Morris & Co., Taken in hand by Blyth Drydock and Shipbuilding, she lost her merchantman status, a flight deck was built on her and she became "*Empire Audacity*", later, just plain "*Audacity*", the world's first escort carrier.

Winston Churchill visited Brown's squadron as they were working up for their first deployment and the Martlets were used to put on an impressive aerial display. Sub-Lieutenant Brown took off on his part of the demonstration and immediately rolled inverted after take-off as part of the show. His engine seized in this awkward position and his Martlet plummeted into the Firth of Forth directly in front of the prime minister. Brown was fished out of the water unharmed.

In 1940, the British approached the United States Navy with the plans of *Audacity*. It was at the time of the exchange of information between the United Kingdom and the United States and the Royal Navy asked for six such vessels to be built. The US Navy secretary, Frank Knox, wrote to the Bureau of Ships on the 10th January 1941, instructing them to proceed, with all haste, in the building of a diesel-powered ship of the C-3 type, or other. 17 days after the letter was sent to the Maritime Commission, the conversion of the SS *Mormacmail* commenced, and by 2nd June 1941 she was ready for service as the USS *Long Island*. She was the first of the "Jeep" carriers and joined the Atlantic Fleet on the 15th July. She was identical in plan to HMS *Audacity* and was the first of 123 for the US Navy and 38 for the Royal Navy as Lend-Lease carriers. The Royal Navy never received USS *Long Island*.

802 Squadron embarked on *Audacity* from Machrihanish after a period of training and the squadron of six Martlets was spilt into two flights and sub-divided into sections of two for combat purposes. One section, Yellow section, was diverted to HMS *Argus* for Operation Benedict, the supply of Hurricanes to Russia. This was during her first convoy, OG74, of 13th September 1941. OG74 was a Gibraltar bound convoy and one FW 200 was shot down by the squadron. On the return voyage, Brown was wounded by enemy return fire, shattering his windscreen and when his Martlet took the wire his face smashed into the instrument panel. Brown admitted that he had not fastened his shoulder straps.

It was during this period that he perfected the head on attack against four-engined bombers. On one flight, pursuing a bomber into cloud, he found himself on a collision course with the enemy. Opening fire at the nose, he killed the pilots and the aircraft plunged into the sea. The nose attack proved to be the Achilles heel of the Condor. HMS *Audacity* lost her charmed life when she was torpedoed and sunk by the U571. One of 73 survivors, Winkle Brown, was saved by his aircrew life preserver.

802 Squadron was then reformed with Sea Hurricanes, but the pattern of life was to change for Eric Brown. His old CO had noticed his outstanding flying abilities and suggested that he would make an excellent test pilot. As a result, he was posted to Farnborough, to test the all-wood Miles M20 stop-gap fighter. This fighter was built around the Miles Master with a fixed undercarriage. It was also powered by the Rolls–Royce Merlin in "power egg" form as found on the Bristol Beaufighter. From there he tested the Sea Hurricane on HMS *Avenger* to determine whether it could be deployed on the new Jeep Carriers. He found that it could. From these test flights there followed a period on Argus as an instructor on Fairey Fulmars. This was in Scottish waters on the Firth of Clyde. On one occasion control of the Fulmar was lost and it was swept to the side of the vessel. The aircraft was left dangling by hook and wire. To his surprise the Fulmar was soon flying. To his relief, the Fulmars were replaced by Sea Hurricanes. He went on to more squadron service and then tested

the new Supermarine Seafire on HMS *Biter*. His first enemy aircraft flight was in a captured Italian Fiat CR42 at RNAS Arbroath.

There was more experimental work to follow, when he was again posted to RAE Farnborough, where there were severe problems with the Fairey Barracuda, including carbon monoxide fumes leaking into the cockpit. When he first saw the Barracuda at Arbroath in 1942, it just did not look right to him. By the time he flew it at Farnborough, five inexplicable fatal crashes had occurred. The accidents occurred mostly in torpedo dropping exercises. As the pilot dropped his torpedo and pulled out, the Barracuda rolled over on to its back and plunged into the sea. Winkle suspected over balance in the rudder and he simulated the manoeuvre at altitude. As soon as he raised the Youngman flaps and kicked on hard rudder the machine went into an inverted dive. Barracuda handling instructions were soon amended and the problems were overcome. At Farnborough he flew many German types, including the Focke Wulf FW 190, FW200, the Me262 and the Ju88, amongst others. He felt that there were three outstanding German aircraft of World War 2, the Me262, the FW190 and the Ju88. By the end of 1943, he had amassed a staggering 1,500 deck landings on 22 different carriers.

At the end of 1943, by then promoted to Lieutenant, Brown progressed from service trials to pure experimental flying. With no formal test pilot training, he was posted to southern Italy to fly captured enemy aircraft. After a few minutes of ground instruction and study, he was sent airborne in a variety of single-engine and multi-engine Italian aircraft. He survived this experience and his impressed commander sent him to the Aerodynamics Flight at Farnborough. In his first month, he flew 13 different aircraft types, consisting of seven entirely new prototypes, including a Focke-Wulf FW 190.

On one trial he had a heart-stopping moment in a Tempest V, JN735. After three runs and flying at over 400 mph, there was a colossal bang from the Sabre engine and the propeller stopped. Oil covered the windscreen and as he descended through the cloud, a fire developed under the engine cowling and along the floor. He bailed out at 1200ft and landed in the middle of a shallow farm pond and had to be rescued from an irate bull by the police and fire brigade. Despite this experience, he considered the Tempest to be a very good aircraft. Another aircraft flown at Farnborough by Brown was the Gloster E.28/39, the first British jet prototype, which he had seen earlier at Cranwell. One out of every three flights of this jet ended in engine failure. The aircraft was powered by Frank Whittle's first operational jet engine from Power Jets.

By the time Brown was involved in testing the E28/39 it was well behind contract due to engine problems and production difficulties at the engine manufacturer, Power Jets. The contract was to produce a jet fighter around the specification, but the target was not met and the first operational British jet fighter became the Gloster Meteor.

Among other memorable aeroplanes he flew was the Miles Libellula canard, which was to be developed into a naval aircraft and ultimately a bomber, but rejected because it had excessive drag. The Morris furniture firm of Glasgow developed much of the wood for this aircraft and other Miles types. He also tested the General Aircraft G.A.L.56 tailless glider. It had very poor flying characteristics and was prone to stall viciously. Brown finally delivered the glider to Lasham airfield and handed it over to Robert Kronfeld, one of the world's most experienced glider pilots. Kronfeld's first flight in the G.A.L.56 ended in a crash which killed him. Kronfeld had escaped the Nazi persecution in Austria and was a senior pilot at the Airborne Forces Experimental Establishment during the war, where he had tested a variety of rotorcraft.

The Miles M52 supersonic aircraft was another wartime design he was involved with. The wing of the M52 was unswept, with very sharp leading and trailing edges. The wing, built with Morris wood, was flown experimentally on a Miles Falcon. This aircraft, because of its sharp wing, was called the "Gillette Falcon". There were great problems with the Miles M52; it was longitudinally unstable and the pilot would have had great difficulty getting out in the event of trouble. It also had a huge take-off run. Ultimately, he never flew it, the project being abandoned before its first flight. At RNAS *Jackdaw*,

Crail, he flew the Blackburn Firebrand strike fighter, with which he was singularly unimpressed.

As the chief naval test pilot at Farnborough, his first major project was to determine the feasibility of landing a twin-engine aircraft on a carrier. The aircraft chosen for this experiment was the twin-engine DH98 Mosquito. Since the Mosquito Mark VI was twice the weight of any aircraft which had landed on a British carrier, a substantial amount of work had to be done to demonstrate this concept. Much work was done on modifying the propellers and the Rolls–Royce Merlin engine for the landing. The propellers were modified as were the propeller hubs. However, Lieutenant Brown quickly completed this project. When he landed on the HMS *Implacable* on 25th March 1944 he performed the first deck landing of a high performance twin-engine aircraft on a carrier. Everything was ideal, except for the fact that the crew had forgotten to reserve him a cabin on the ship for the night! As he contemplated his first major flight test milestone, he fell asleep on the carrier's wardroom settee.

In 1944 a radical project emerged from the Admiralty in the form of a flexible deck fitted to an aircraft carrier upon which jet aircraft could land without an undercarriage. The landing technique was pioneered on an experimental deck at Farnborough. The first flight of the modified Sea Vampire resulted in an accident, but in spite of this over 200 landings were successfully made by pilots, some with varying skills and some of whom had never flown a jet before. Eric Brown made forty eight successful landings on the flexible deck by 1948, the deck having been fitted to the carrier vessel HMS *Warrior*.

The flexible deck was not adopted. Peace brought about other developments to aircraft and aircraft carriers; the angled deck had been introduced, as was the steam catapult and the mirror deck landing system.

His most unusual flight took place at Renfrew aerodrome during the war. He had delivered a Grumman Tigercat from Farnborough to Blackburn/Lockheed at the airfield and there, in a hangar, he found a captured Japanese Mitsubishi Zero, possibly on its way to the USA or Farnborough. He organised a test flight and flew this delightful aircraft round Loch Lomond and the Trossachs and back to the airfield. He was very impressed with the aircraft's flying characteristics, but not so with its lack of armour and self-sealing fuel tanks.

With the end of the war in Europe, he was posted to Germany, where, amongst others, he interrogated Herman Goering, the leading, surviving Nazi. He found him to be highly articulate, intelligent and with an ability to manipulate every question and answer - "A slippery customer", said Brown. Goering told him, under interview, that he felt that the Battle of Britain had been a draw. To Brown, that was an astonishing conclusion. He also interrogated Himmler and discovered that, as Controller of Aircraft Quality and Control, he had had Werner von Braun, the rocket pioneer, arrested. Another prominent aviation pioneer he interviewed was Hanna Reitsch. She was afraid of the Odessa or Steel Helmet, whose threat had to be taken seriously. (These were ex-Nazi military, now civilians.)

Brown's fluency in German was a great help to the Allies. He met and conversed with German aircraft manufacturers, such as Heinkel, and other test pilots. He also interviewed two exceptional pilots, Fritz Wendel, of Messerschmitt and Kurt Tank, the designer of the Focke Wulf Fw190 fighter. Tank carried out the first flights of all the aircraft he had designed and was another ardent Nazi. Hanna Reitsch seemed to him to hover on the fringes of aircraft research in Germany. She was a political appointee, a consultant test pilot for the Luftwaffe, and Brown felt that she was heartily disliked by most other German test pilots. She had also tried to fly Hitler out of Berlin in 1945, when the city was collapsing under the attacks of the Soviet Army. Interestingly, she was also an acquaintance of Neil Morris, of Morris Furniture, Glasgow. Neil B. Morris was also involved in early British helicopter development. Hanna Reitsch test flew a piloted version of the V1 flying bomb and Brown felt that she, too, was a very enthusiastic Nazi.

Eric Brown was also to meet the chief test pilot of Arado, Joachim Carl. He taught him the flight characteristics of the Arado 234 Blitz.

The Blitz was a very fine reconnaissance bomber and it was also the first dedicated jet-propelled bomber in world service.

At the end of the war, Winkle Brown was put in charge of the Enemy Aircraft Flight at RAE Farnborough and flew 55 different types of captured German aircraft. At the German airfield of Grove, later to become the NATO base of Karup, he was intrigued to find that many German pilots had fled there from the Russians, with their aircraft. His first attempt to fly an Arado 234 jet led to turbine failure. On inspection, the defective engine was found to have been sabotaged. His next Arado 234 was more serviceable. He was to deliver it from Sola in Norway to Farnborough, with a refuelling stop at Brussels, Melsbroek. He found the view from the cockpit very uncomfortable in fog and he had to constantly monitor the fuel state.

A different type altogether was the Messerschmitt Me163 Komet rocket interceptor, which he flew in Germany and at Farnborough. By subterfuge, he managed to obtain fuel for one Me163 flight. With the help of the surviving Komet pilots he flew the machine, "196859", in Germany over Husum, Schleswig-Holstein on 10th June 1945, in a flight he described as "Fantastic". He took the machine to 32,000 feet. He had flown three towed flights to 20000 feet, the tug being an Me110.

Brown had promised the German pilots that he would not reveal the powered flight publicly until the last of the Komet pilots had died. Knowledge of this flight was also hidden from the public by the security services.

Fourteen days later he flew two Russian fighters. These were the Mig3 and the La7. He described the Mig as a "Useful little fighter" and the La7 as, "Satisfactory, but with poor equipment". Earlier, on the 23rd June 1945, he flew the Il2, describing it as, "Rough as old socks". On that same day he flew the Il4 but made no comment on how it handled.

Echoing Hannah Reitsch, Winkle Brown described the Komet as a sensational aeroplane to fly, of extremely unusual design, outstanding performance and highly efficient in its interceptor role. But the aircraft required a very high standard of flying skill to survive the appalling hazards of fuel and engine safety; in short, it was a death trap. Rocket powered aircraft had been banned by the Allies from flying in post-war Germany and that ban continued at Farnborough. The Farnborough trials were carried out without power, the Me163 being towed as a glider to altitude by a Spitfire. The Komet was to play a major data-gathering role for a planned, point defence, supersonic fighter, but the trial was cut short when the nose skid collapsed during a high-speed landing at Wittering. Winkle once again miraculously escaped serious injury, but the aircraft was a write-off.

On July 2, 1965 Captain Brown was a guest at the Munich Aviation Museum, when a refurbished Me163, for which a rocket motor had been supplied by the RAE, was unveiled in the presence of its designer and test pilots. These were the aircraft designer, Dr Alexander Lippisch and the production leader, Dr Willy Messerschmitt, the designer of the rocket motor, Dr Helmut Walther and two leading German rocket test pilots, Fritz Wendel and Rudolf Opitz. Brown had remembered seeing an Me163 rocket motor lying in a Farnborough hangar and when he mentioned this, the engine was found exactly where he said it would be.

Another remarkable experience was to fly the giant Blohm und Voss Bv222 six diesel-engined flying boat from Trondheim in Norway to Calshot. He had never flown a flying boat of this size before and he had to depend on German assistance. On take-off the co-pilot, a Luftwaffe major, tried to wreck the boat. He was summarily dealt with and the rest of the flight was fairly uneventful.

Another diversion at Farnborough was a catapult launch in a Grumman Avenger. When it flew off, the wings folded as it left the catapult. Fortunately for Winkle, this rugged American machine dropped to the ground and rolled across the aerodrome with its undercarriage still intact. There was also a very dangerous Seafire flight off a catapult. On firing the rockets the carriage still remained attached to the fuselage, but he survived.

He also recalled being very impressed by the highly unorthodox Dornier Do335 Arrow twin-engined fighter. This was the Luftwaffe's fastest piston-engined fighter, which was fitted with ejection seats. Winkle Brown told the macabre story of how the two prototypes had crashed, the pilots failing to eject properly, their bodies being found without arms. The hood jettison lever was attached directly to the canopy itself so, when the hood blew off, so did the pilot's arms.

In December 1945 he carried out the world's first landing of a jet aircraft, a Sea Vampire, aboard an aircraft carrier at sea (HMS *Ocean*.) For this he was awarded an OBE. At the end of the war he elected to stay in the Royal Navy and took a four year short service commission and remained at Farnborough for test flying. Much of his early work involved compressibility problems which were beginning to arise with such aircraft as the Spitfire, Mustang, Tempest and the de Havilland D.H.108 tailless research aircraft.

He was not at all impressed with the Avro Tudor airliner, feeling that it needed a complete redesign. The Avro Tudor was an offshoot of the Avro Manchester/Lancaster/Lincoln/Shackleton series. This was in preparation for work with the jet-powered Avro Ashton. He was also deeply involved in many rotary wing trials with early helicopters. On occasion he would fly the Sikorsky Hoverfly through smoke generated by a captured Fieseler Storch to study the blade characteristics.

In 1947 he was appointed CO of the Farnborough Aerodynamics Flight and received the Air Force Cross for his work on high speed and rotary-wing research flying. He also received the Boyd Trophy and the King's Commendation for Valuable Service in the Air. He was also granted a permanent commission in 1949. After six years at Farnborough he was posted to a front-line naval squadron at the School of Naval Air Warfare, St Merryn, Cornwall.

Just before he left for Farnborough he was invited to fly the Saunders-Roe SRA/1 jet flying-boat fighter. After a briefing by Geoffrey Tyson, Saunders Roe's chief test pilot, he took off. Before landing was warned that the wind direction had changed and to look out for flotsam. Low on fuel, he had to land immediately, but the flying-boat struck a wooden spar, which hit the starboard float, ripping it off. The wing hit the water and the flying-boat cartwheeled.

Fortunately, on this occasion, he had flown with an open cockpit, but when he got out of the cockpit, he found himself trapped under the inverted wing. After several attempts, he surfaced, utterly exhausted. Luckily, Geoffrey Tyson saw his predicament and he dived, fully dressed, into the sea to pull Brown's life preserver inflation toggle.

In December he returned to 802 Sqn at RNAS *Culdrose* as Senior Pilot, embarking on HMS *Vengeance*. This brought his total of deck landings to 2,000, one of which ended in a barrier crash, when the elevators of his Sea Fury were jammed by a loose bolt. In 1950 HMS *Indomitable* made the first visit of a British carrier to Sweden, and Brown formed an aerobatic display team to put on a show for the Swedes.

His most interesting assignment was an exchange posting to the Flight Test Division of the US Naval Air Test Center at Patuxent River, Maryland. It was there that he saw the remains of a British Westland Whirlwind fighter on the river bank. At this time there was a free exchange of information with the US Navy, which had been established during the war. At the time, the Americans were heavily committed to the Korean War and very long hours were worked at Patuxent, testing the Grumman Panther, McDonnell Banshee, Douglas Skyknight and Grumman Bearcat etc. In February 1952 he carried out a remarkable test, by taking off in a Grumman Panther from the newly invented British steam catapult, installed in the carrier HMS *Perseus*, which was moored in Philadelphia Navy Yard. (*The catapult was designed by C.C. Mitchell of Brown Brothers and Company, Scotland. Design work had started in 1948. The Perseus tests were funded by the United States. Eric Brown had worked closely with Mitchell on its development.*)

It was necessary for the wind to blow from bow to stern, but on that day the wind blew in the opposite direction. Winkle decided to go ahead anyway and a completely successful test launch was made. There, he had the opportunity to discuss with the Americans the angled flight deck concept. The Americans were very impressed with the design and went to work immediately. Within nine months, the carrier *Antietam* was at sea with an angled flight deck. The Americans were also very impressed by the British use of heavy aircraft and jets operating from carriers. These heavy types for both navies were capable of delivering nuclear stores.

In the United States he broke the sound barrier for the first time in a North American F-86 Sabre and in 1953 he received his watch-keeping certificate during his service in the anti-submarine frigate HMS *Rocket*, out of Londonderry.

In November 1953 he went to Lossiemouth as CO of 804 Sqn, being promoted Commander in December. In 1954 he trained an aerobatic team of Sea Hawks, which included a seven-aircraft loop in its repertoire. He then received a posting to RNAS *Brawdy*, where, in 1956, he had a very strange encounter with a UFO, chasing it across the country. He photographed it and stuck a print in his logbook. But this sighting, as with so many other sightings made by highly responsible and intelligent pilots, remains enigmatic. From *Brawdy* he went to a Joint Services staff course at the RAF College, Manby.

In July 1957 he made his first supersonic flight in a British aeroplane, a Hunter F4, eight years after achieving Mach 0.985 in the D.H. 108. Later, in December 1957, he was invited to go to Germany to establish and train the new German Naval Air Arm forming at Kiel and Schleswig, where he was given his own personal transport, a Percival Pembroke. This was the first aircraft of the new German Navy flying unit and was kept in pristine condition. In 1958 he became head of the British Naval Air Mission to Germany, a post which enabled him to keep his hand in at test flying for Focke-Wulf. It was at this time that he attended a funeral for a former U Boat captain, but unexpectedly, Grand Admiral Karl Doenitz attended as well, Brown being the only British officer present. When Doenitz appeared he was surrounded by enthusiastic German officers, much to Winkle Brown's embarrassment. In Germany he was amazed to see how its industry had recovered from the devastation of the Second World War.

Invited to a party with his wife, Brown was the only British officer present. As the night wore on, the German Naval officers became more boisterous. Suddenly curtains were drawn back and a door revealed. Everyone marched through the doorway, including Winkle and his wife. He was astounded to see the walls and tables decorated with Nazi memorabilia. Even more disturbing were trophies from British and Allied sunken vessels. The festivities continued and when they left Winkle notified the appropriate authorities.

He spent a large part of the first half of 1958 working with German naval leadership and training German Navy's new pilots, many of whom had combat experience. He also worked closely with Rear Admiral Wagner of the German Naval Staff, the last surviving signatory of Germany's unconditional surrender. Clearly, Brown's role required "great diplomacy and tact". His team spent a large amount of time in Britain, helping the German pilots train on Hawker Sea Hawks and Fairey Gannets. They were also being trained on the Bristol Sycamore helicopter.

Brown led the first operational unit of the German Navy Air Arm onto German soil from Britain in June 1958; it was a great day for the resurrected Marineflieger. There was an even a greater day when the squadrons were finally assigned to NATO in 1960.

In Germany he continued his test flying. The Focke-Wulf Company had lost its chief test pilot and permission was granted for him to work with the company. He had come full circle; from flying the FW 190 and other Focke–Wulf types in WW2 to testing their new post war aircraft.

In 1960 he was promoted to Captain, and in 1961 was appointed to the Directorate of Naval Air Warfare. He joined a team planning the new 53,000-ton carrier of a radically new design, the *CVA-01*, under the aegis of the Conservative government of the time, and he was responsible for designing the aircraft deck layout. It was under his influence that the Royal Navy ordered the McDonnell Phantom. He was also advisor on aircraft accidents. In 1964 the newly-elected Labour government decided to abandon carriers and carrier aviation altogether, and *CVA-01* was cancelled.

He was appointed Naval Attaché in Bonn, West Germany and this was followed by command of the Royal Naval Air Station at Lossiemouth, where he had access to a Grumman Hellcat and a Fairey

Fulmar. Legend has him secreting the dark blue Hellcat in a hangar at a satellite airfield, away from the prying eyes of officialdom. He was awarded the CBE in the 1970 Honours List.

At Lossiemouth he made his final service flight in a Westland Whirlwind helicopter. The engine failed and he had to make a forced landing in the snow. He landed successfully by engaging the tailskid in a wire fence. He left the Royal Navy on 12th March 1970, to become chief executive of the British Helicopter Advisory Board, a body which promoted helicopter operations in the UK. He continued to write and went on the lecture circuit, including a presentation to the Scottish Astro Cosmic Society at Coatbridge. His articles in aviation magazines were always enthusiastically received. His first article was on the Me163 in Air Enthusiast, September 1972. He was also a guest on BBC Radio's "Desert Island Discs" and from this broadcast we found that he sang with Glenn Miller during the war and later secretly met the Soviet cosmonauts Yuri Gagarin and Valentina Tereshkova in London at the Admiralty. He also served as president of the Royal Aeronautical Society from 1982-83. His last flight was at the controls of a French helicopter in 1994.

Captain Eric "Winkle" Brown died aged 97, on 21st February 2016 at East Surrey Hospital in Redhill, Surrey, after a short illness. R.I.P.

A Westland Whirlwind helicopter

Overall assessment of some WW II aircraft

1. **Sea Gladiator**. One of the greatest biplane fighters ever: outperformed and outgunned, but never outmanoeuvred.
2. **Swordfish**. An obsolete design which could only perform in air superiority. It possessed good handling qualities, but performed poorly.
3. **Skua.** As a fighter it had little hope of success. An effective dive bomber.
4. **Sea Hurricane**. A great dogfighter, effective bomber interceptor with outstanding manoeuvrability, but outclassed by more modern enemy fighters.
5. **Albacore**. An anachronism ,with poor performance, poor defensive armament and manoeuvrability.
6. **Wildcat**. A great asset for the Fleet Air Arm, a potent fighter and a superb deck landing aircraft.
7. **Barracuda**. Performance pathetic, but an effective dive bomber.
8. **Seafire**. A land aeroplane for shipboard use, with the ditching characteristics of a brick. Great to fly and fight.
9. **Fulmar**. As a fighter, well below average with a punch, reasonably manoeuvrable, with good endurance.

Luftwaffe Aircraft

1. **Ju88**. An outstanding airframe, a pilot's aeroplane, first and last.
2. **Bucker Jungmeister**. An aerobatic gem.
3. **Arado Ar234B**. Beautiful streamlined shape.
4. **Blohm & Voss BV222**. An impressive monster of a flying boat.
5. **Fieseler Storch**. A virtuoso of slow flight with unique take-off and landing abilities.
6. **Focke-Wulf FW190**. A superb fighter with an outstanding rate of roll.

7. **Heinkel He162**. Had superb aerodynamic controls.
8. **Junkers Ju 87**. A true vertical dive-bomber and deadly effective.
9. **Messerschmitt Bf109G**. I was not impressed.
10. **Messerschmitt Me163**. A tool of desperation.
11. **Messerschmitt Me262**. A quantum jump in fighter performance.
12. **Siebel Si 204D**. Excellent utilitarian aircraft.
13. **Fw 200 Condor/Kurier**. All the shortcomings that were to be expected of a converted airliner.
14. **FW 189.** "The Flying Eye". An aura that defies analysis.

Eric "Winkle" Brown, selected bibliography

1. "Wings on my Sleeve", Captain Eric "Winkle" Brown, Weidenfeld & Nicolson, 2006.
2. "Wings on my Sleeve", A Star Book, 1984
3. "Duels in the Sky", Naval Institute Press, 1988.
4. "Wings of the Luftwaffe", Crecy Publishing Ltd. 2010.
5. "Testing for Combat", Airlife, 1994
6. "Dawn of the Carrier Jet". Article, Air International, Vol 28, No 1, January 1985

Air International/Air Enthusiast part "Viewed from the Cockpit" Series

September 1972, Me163 Komet: **July 1974,** Ju 87 Stuka: **Sept 1974,** FW200 Condor: **March 1982,** Grumman Panther: **May 1982,** Supermarine Attacker: **July 1982,** Grumman Cougar: **October 1982,** de Havilland Sea Hornet: **December 1982,** Hawker Sea Hawk: **February 1976,** FW190: **December 1976,** Fieseler Storch: **April 1975,** Heinkel He177: **July 1975,** Heinkel He219: **January 1985,** Dawn of the Carrier Jet: **May 1977,** Fairey Barracuda:

August 1977, Fairey Fulmar: **November 1977**, Blackburn Skua: **February 1976**, Vampire on a Trampoline: **August 1978**, Blackburn Firebrand: **August 1984**, Grumman Tigercat: **September 1980**, Hawker SeaFury: **January 1973**, Dornier 335: **August 1979**, Fairey Firefly: **March 1978**, Fairey Albacore – list not complete, volumes published June to July.

Grumman Hellcat being batted down, HMS Ravager, Firth of Clyde, Scotland October 1944

Transcript of a presentation given to the United States Navy

POST-WAR AIRCRAFT CARRIER INNOVATIONS AND THEIR

INFLUENCE ON MODERN DEVELOPMENTS IN CARRIER

AVIATION

(1987)

(Images not suitable for publication)

I would like to first of all thank you for the invitation to this illustrious establishment and also for the privilege of being asked to address you here this afternoon. Now, it was my intention to talk about just post-war carrier innovations, but thinking it over, I have to lead in a little from the war times, so we're going to cover a bit of ground at fairly high speed this afternoon.

I would like to say to you that, in my opinion, Advanced Technology is essentially development of the potential of innovatory ideas. Some of these, incredibly simple in concept, very often are followed by circumstantial pressures such as a crucial war-time situation or a peace-time budgetary cut, which bring them to fruition. It can be either type of thing and this is all splendidly illustrated in the area of aircraft carrier aviation, where the objectives are to enhance the performance of carrier aircraft, while keeping the carrier flight deck compatible with safe operation. Because of the numerous limiting parameters that dictate carrier size, technical problems concerning the safe operation of aircraft mainly relate to short take-off and landing. So what I am going to do is examine these in a chronological order.

Now, your President Franklin D. Roosevelt and our Prime Minister, Winston Churchill, both agreed that if World War Two was to be progressed to a successful outcome, the most critical factor was first to win the battle of the Atlantic and keep open this vital supply line that was being harassed continuously by German U-Boats and reconnaissance aircraft. It was essential, therefore, that our convoys had to be provided with air cover and so the idea of the escort carrier was born. And this is the first of these such vessels that was used operationally and is probably the smallest aircraft carrier ever to be so used. It was named HMS *Audacity*. It was, in fact, a captured German banana boat, and it was brought to Britain and the top sliced off and a flight deck put on. The flight deck was only 420 feet long by 60 feet wide. There was no hangar; it had a deck-park for 6 or 8 fighters. There were only 2 arrester wires and a third wire which was connected to the barrier, so if you caught the third wire, which was colourfully called the "for Christ's sake wire", you then pulled the barrier down so you were able to run over it. Now this was a highly successful vessel. It only did 3 months of operations before it was sunk and yet, at the end of its time, Grand Admiral Doenitz himself said that "the appearance of this type of vessel was the biggest worry that was ever introduced into my operational command". Now, its success was largely made by virtue of the type of aircraft that was used, which happily was provided by your great country under the Lend-Lease situation, and the Grumman Wildcat had the requisite power and performance to operate successfully on such a small platform.

There was no British aircraft that really could have done the job at that time. So much has to be said for this wonderful little machine, and, of course, it introduced something quite innovatory to us in the form of the "sting" which you have here at the back end of the machine. One has to admit that the performance of the Wildcat, good as it was against certain types of weather, was not good enough to cope with the fighters currently in the European theatre and so the British Admiralty turned to look at higher performance aircraft which, of course, were land-based. Since they had no ability to operate from a carrier, we had to resort to devices such as this. Now, here you have what is called the CAM ship (catapult aircraft merchant ship), and that is our Hawker Hurricane high performance fighter on a 65 feet long rocket catapult.

It attained 70 knots in that 65 feet and was launched whenever our convoy was approached by an enemy bomber or a reconnaissance aircraft or, indeed, an enemy fighter if it got close to shore. The snag in this was of course that the plane, unless you were close to shore, was lost and the pilot had to bail out, because the Hurricane had the ditching characteristics of a submarine and therefore you had to part company with it. We also tried the same thing with the Spitfire. Here you see the Spitfire on the rocket catapult. In all these pictures I am the pilot, I have to tell you, so if any mistakes are made, they are all mine. You will notice we had a very cumbersome method of catapulting in those days, which was a cradle on a trolley and you had to have four weighty spools, two on each side of the aircraft, fore and aft, to fit into the slots of this type of cradle. The trolley had at its front end two prongs which went into two tubes filled with water and these tubes had a fibre disk at their open end and the 10 feet long prongs penetrated the tube and this arrested the trolley in a distance of 10 feet.

I'm going to show you now what happened when a chap forgot to put the water in one day. The trolley smashes through the tubes and remains attached to the aircraft with the rockets still going strong, but fortunately you see the trolley beginning to depart from me. It stayed with me for quite a few feet before it finally came away. Now, as I said, these land based aircraft could not be brought off a carrier by any normal means, so if we begin to operate them and convert them to be able to have arrester gear they had to be assisted by rocket take-off gear. These were fitted, two rockets on each side of the aircraft to give the requisite short take-off on the smaller type of carriers. It was a good idea also to have an aircraft fitted with this sort of rocket gear sitting on deck for deck interception; that is to say, if you got very, very limited time warning of the approach of an enemy aircraft the fighter was immediately available to take-off instantly. Fire the rockets and away you go. Now the alternative to using rocket assisted take-off was of course the hydraulic catapult which you will see here. This is a Hellcat, a Grumman Hellcat, and again you introduced us to something entirely new, innovatory, which we latched onto at once.

That is the two or three point launching method you had, where the strop attaches to a shuttle in the slot of the catapult, then into a single hook or two hooks under the belly of the aircraft. So we got rid of that cumbersome trolley system, which I showed you earlier on and came onto this type of catapult. Now all these systems were useful in their own way, but they did show that the problem related to the fact that we required more power for take-off. Fundamentally that was the shortcoming and one of the obvious things to do was to turn to the twin engine aircraft, where usually an excess of power was available, and we had in Britain at that time an aircraft called the De Havilland Mosquito. This was a very high performance fighter bomber, and we decided we would convert this and make a deck landing with it, and here I am making the first such landing. You see it's quite a big aircraft, and we thought at the time, like Professor Bock stated, that this was the first twin engine landing of an aircraft on a carrier, but in fact it proved not to be. It was the first operational aircraft, but actually the USN had made 8 or 10 landings as far back as August 1939 with an experimental, rather a civilian-looking type of aircraft called the XJO. But the Mosquito was a very fast machine, and its normal landing speed ashore was 125 mph. Well, it was quite obvious there was no carrier gear around that was going to take this sort of thing, and we were about the first to use the lift control available in the engine power and the propellers by making the approach at a very high power setting, and in fact the first touchdown which was just about to be made here was at 78 mph. Now to get an aircraft that lands normally at 125 mph down to that speed, I had to have a lot of power on, and therefore required fairly big draggy flaps as you see, and these flaps were specifically enlarged for this purpose. I should tell you that I managed to get this aircraft off in 52 yards, and it's a 20 thousand pound aircraft. Fifty-two yards with a wind speed of 34 knots, that is a combined wind speed and ship speed of 34 knots. So it really got off like a scalded cat. A big advantage of course was the view that the twin engine plane produced, but it gave also 1 or 2 snags, the main snag being how do you cope with an asymmetric landing if you lose 1 engine? This was an extremely difficult problem and one that was not readily solvable. The other problem was the span of the aircraft was such that in order to take off it had to be ranged with the port wheel very near the port edge of the deck so the starboard wing tip would avoid the island, and since the natural swing with the torque of the propellers was to port, there was very, very little margin for error on take-off. The aircraft was never, therefore, used operationally because we really couldn't solve the asymmetric problem, but I did about 30 or 40 landings with it and we really had no trouble during these landings. We therefore went to a hotted-up version of this called the Sea Hornet. This is a single-seat version of the two-seat Mosquito and it was probably one of the most overpowered aircraft ever built. These Rolls-Royce engines had handed propellers going in opposite rotation so that no swing problem occurred. The view of course, as always, was magnificent with the twin. This thing had magnificent performance on one engine, and we did try to get down to single engine landings on a carrier, but time really was too short and we had to give it up, but the aircraft went into operational service because it had such long range that in the event of engine failure it almost certainly could make shore. It was booked for operations in the Far East at the end of the Japanese war and, therefore, had to have long range, but it was a remarkably fine aircraft. It is so overpowered I used to have an aerobatic display on this where I did a loop on both engines, a loop on one engine and finished up with a loop on no engines—always makes fun. The only thing you've got to put a little trust in is to be able to unfeather when you're coming off the bottom of the loop with no engines, otherwise, you're going to look rather silly! The advent of the jet in naval applications at the end of WWII looked as if it might solve a lot of our problems, certainly performance-wise, but it brought as many headaches as it brought relief from some of the other problems.

Here I am making the first jet landing on an aircraft carrier in December 1945 and once again a magnificent view as you can see. However, the take-off performance left much to be desired because, of course, we had lost lift control which was provided by the propeller and the piston engine combination. Because of this, a very different type of approach had to be made, and the one I had devised at that time we called constant- attitude and constant-rate-of-descent. You wanted to have as few variables involved as possible because lift control was so poor. Now that system is still used today. There has been no change from that. I will show you the actual approach. Here is an approach being made in that constant- attitude and constant-rate-of-descent onto the deck. One thing, of course, the jet did solve was the asymmetric problem. In other words, if you had a twin jet, (This is not of course. This is a single engine jet and these are just double intakes.) but, if you had a jet engine you could bring it closer to the fuselage on either side and the loss of one power unit meant that you had very little offset asymmetric thrust and that problem was indeed very well solved.

Now at this time a rash of new ideas begin to come into our minds about the operation of jet aircraft and one of them, of course, was that the barrier had to be redesigned. The normal barrier, as you know, was a solid piece of cross- stranded wire and in the jet aircraft you have no piston engine and propeller situation ahead of you; you sit very close to the accident, so the idea was to have the stranded nylon cords shown here and the nose just penetrated through them, and they wound themselves around the wing and brought the aircraft to a halt. A tedious operation, of course, was when you had mixed squadrons of jets and piston engines, because you had to have both types of barrier operating aboard. Therefore, one of our first thoughts was, how do we get rid of this barrier situation. Here you have the normal carrier deck, you have the arresting wires, and normally as you know, we have two barriers to arrest anything, just in case one went through the first one. We also thought that perhaps we could have the aircraft approaching onto a single wire. We gave up the idea of the other two wires and we were going to have a single wire and a rubber deck, and remove the undercarriage from the aircraft because the undercarriage of the naval aircraft usually represents about seven percent of the all- up weight. So in one fell swoop we hoped to get rid of the problem of the barrier because we were not going to approach at a normal deck landing speed of about 1.1 to 1.15 times the stalling speed. The idea was to approach at 1.25 to 1.3 times the stalling speed and pick up the single wire and pitch on to the rubber deck. There was not going to be a barrier—that was also eliminated. This was the first idea and I'll show you the actual thing in action as it really came to be. Here you have the single wire; it was, of course, much higher than the normal wire which is approximately nine inches above the deck. In this case it is about three feet above the deck. Coming in at about 1.25 times the stalling speed, there is the pick-up and there is the landing, flopping onto a rubber mat, beneath which are five layers of firemen's hoses athwart ships, at low pressure, pressures varying from six pounds per square inch to two and a half.

This rubber mat was the equivalent of the outer cover of a normal automobile tyre. It was stretched under tension from both sides. Friction on the mat was very, very low, indeed: a very low co-efficient of friction. Now if you missed the wire, the idea was you had enough power on at 1.3 Vg to just carry on in a straight run, and have another go. The barrier we had was, in fact, an emergency barrier. If the time came you had so many goes you were running out of fuel, it had to be done, but in the normal operation, there was no intention of having a barrier associated with it at all. Now this idea of a flexible deck led us into another thought at this time. We thought this system is not really terribly practical because it's too radical in the sense that you would have to have ashore a lot of these rubber mat landing devices, so it was not too practical. However, we were intrigued by the fact we were not faced with barrier problems, because the barrier accidents in carrier aviation really are extremely high and extremely costly. So we were inevitably led into this thought: the angled deck. We thought the only problem with the flexible deck was you couldn't have a deck park ahead of it and we really wanted a deck park, so we thought well, why don't we just swing the landing area a bit and this is precisely what was done. We started off with five and one half degrees and when I brought the idea from Farnborough, where we had just dreamed it up, to Patuxent River in 1951(1952), your people, with your usual phenomenal speed, latched onto it and you actually had one operating before we did. We had only painted one on one of our carriers, but we hadn't built the actual deck on. In fact there you see it, just painted on a normal deck.

This gave us the answer, of course, to getting rid of the barrier, and reducing the accident rate incredibly. But nothing is perfect, and there were two snags with it. One is this chunk of real estate on the front quarter, doing nothing—wasted space. The other is there are certain problems lining up with the angle deck in bad weather. The first thing a pilot sees when he breaks into visibility range of a carrier in bad weather is the wake of the ship, and of course, the wake of a ship is dead astern and in this case you have to do a swift turn, if that is your guideline, to nine degrees in some cases, so that was not a perfect solution either. But nevertheless, it's one that stayed with us, and will remain with us, until something better is dreamt up. Now, at this particular time, we had, as I said, a rash of other ideas. One of them was a steam catapult. The steam catapult replaced the hydraulic catapult and it had this advantage; it was using a source of energy which was available and going to waste anyway: the ship's own steam. It also was much lighter than the hydraulic catapult and took up less space. It gave smoother acceleration, but a higher g at the end of the run, and when we came over to demonstrate, again when I was at Patuxent, we sent HMS *Perseus* over here and I gave the first demonstration to your Navy in Philadelphia Navy Yard. We were tied up alongside, and the first launch I made in an F9F-3 was with an 8 knot tail wind and the end speed of the aircraft was 142 knots, so that shows you the performance of this catapult. It really was a quantum step forward.

The other idea that came about at this time of course, was what we called the deck mirror landing sight. I think you now call it a Fresnel lens, or something of this order, but basically it is a light datum, with a meatball light source on the mirror, and the pilot, of course, if he's in the perfect angle at that constant- attitude, constant-rate-of-descent will have the meatball lined up with the datum line. If he gets low, this is shown by the position of the meatball which gives a mandatory signal. He must obey the signal therefore by bringing the meatball up by bringing his aircraft up; vice-versa if he's high it will show high and he must bring the meatball down by bringing his aircraft down. This system got rid of a very, very vulnerable human factor, the LSO or deck landing control officer. I say this with the hope that no ex-LSO or ex-DLC officers are here. They only compounded the problems of deck landing in my opinion, because it is a very, very difficult job to do. I'm not saying they didn't do a wonderful job, but it was far from a perfect job. You had a different system from us; your LSO gave advisory signals, whereas ours gave mandatory signals. Both systems had equal drawbacks, so getting rid of the LSO I think was very useful. LSOs are still used, of course, as back-ups to this mirror system, so, provided they are well trained, they can be an asset, but I really was referring to the war time situation when any pilot who was around and spare was just put on to be the LSO, and this is no way to run a railroad at all, and it certainly didn't pay off dividends during war time.

While we were looking for methods of shortening takeoff, I began a series of trials at Farnborough and Sir Frank Whittle will remember these very well. First trials we were doing were on reheat on the jet engine—fairly basic at that time, just injecting fuel into the jet pipe and letting it catch alight there. It was done in a twin-engine jet aircraft which was a single-seat aircraft, but we built a cockpit behind my cockpit where we had a scientist who controlled the experiment, and when he recognized we were cooking too much he cut the fuel supply off—not to the main engine, but just to the reheat system. Pretty crude, but it was the first step towards full reheat and of course, as you're well aware, reheat is now one of the best methods of reducing take-off distance.

Now, we've been through the normal standard deck, we've been through the flexible deck, we've been through the angled deck, was there anything left? Well, here we had an idea that was revolutionary in design. This is CVA-01, which was never built, but I had charge of the think tank that devised this carrier layout and, in fact, the keel was laid and it was going to be built, when a change of government from Conservative to Labour killed it stone dead, because they had decided that Britain was no longer going to get involved in fixed wing carrier aviation. But the idea was fundamentally a parallel deck system. In other words, you had a landing lane, and a take-off lane and they were quite separate and parallel. They weren't strictly parallel purely because of the physical limitations of the width of the carrier, which was 184 feet, and within that we, in fact, had to angle the landing lane 2 and 3/4 degrees. But the idea was that you landed on down this deck, unhooked, taxied out and taxied up along the outboard side of the island. This was a big island (I'll describe it in a minute) up to a point aft of the structure where you were re-armed and refuelled, folded your wings, and taxied back down the inboard side of the island onto the 250 foot steam catapult. There was also a third 250 foot steam catapult here. The island was 200 feet long, and was set back 420 feet from the bow of the ship. This distance and size was determined after extensive wind tunnel tests. All the vehicles which were normally cluttering the flight deck were kept inside an arch on the island which housed these vehicles without any trouble at all. There were two lifts, one in the centre deck for'ard and a deck-edge lift aft. The circulatory flow system meant really that the deck should always be uncluttered and the advantage of course was that we got rid of the worst of the sterile area on the front quarter, which was kept specifically for the rescue helicopter. The other problem of the lining up was reduced of course considerably when you only have an angle of 2 and 3/4 degrees involved. We only had 4 arrest wires, and they were set much farther up the deck than normal for the constant-rate-of-descent type approach. The ship had a top speed of 28 knots, it was 53,000 tons and at that time, in 1960, would have cost £53 million, a thousand pounds sterling per ton and it is a great shame it never went anywhere. We gave the idea over to your people, and whether you ever will do anything with it I don't know, because it's quite a revolutionary change, of course, to build a whole new concept of operating. It was also fitted with a very interesting type of arrester gear. This was a water spray arrester gear. Along the ship's side, under the deck, are very long tubes filled with water, and a piston in each tube connected to an arrester wire. When the arrester wire is caught the piston is pulled along the length of the tube. Since there are hundreds of little perforated holes in the tube, the water is ejected through these holes over the side of the ship, and that is how the energy is dissipated to reduce the landing speed and the pull-out of the aircraft.

The pull-out of this gear was constant for any landing speed or any landing weight within the performance envelope of the gear, so it was a very, very useful gear. It was installed eventually on HMS *Ark Royal* and used there; so there are records of its usage.

Well, this type of ship would have been the last fixed- wing carrier we built, because as you know the helicopter was beginning to come very much into its own in naval aviation, and vertical take-off and landing was taking up everyone's attention. At the same time vertical take-off and landing was made possible on the fixed wing aspect by virtue of vectored thrust and we had the Harrier come into being. So we had a new type of carrier, which was built shortly after CVA-01 was cancelled. And in order to bamboozle the politicians, we called it a "*Through Deck Cruiser*". That is in fact its official title. But of course it's obviously a small aircraft carrier. Here you have the Harrier lined up for vertical take-off and landing type of operation. That was also simplified with a very, very simple device called the "Ski Jump", which you see here- a ramp going up to a maximum of about 8 degrees angle. Provided you have a short take-off run, you can increase the load enormously in a V/STOL aircraft. You can increase it even further if you can produce the energy here to throw it off the end into the air at an angle of attack which otherwise would have to have been achieved by rotation by the pilot. So this is the stage where we are today.

Now you, with your nuclear carriers, of course, still have magnificent fixed wing aircraft aboard, also mixed up with a content of helicopters inevitably. I hope that these will go on for a very long time, because whatever one says, there is no substitute for the high performance fixed wing airplane. We learned this in the Falklands where we had the Harrier, which did a very good job, but because of short range it had to wait until the enemy got to it before we could nail him. If we had had Phantoms, F-4s as we had in the *Ark Royal*, we could have gone out and nailed them half way between the Argentine and the Falklands, so there are very big differences made there. Also, the absence of a fixed wing carrier meant that we had no airborne early warning. That was our biggest deficiency. It was something that, in fact, was a critical factor in the Falklands campaign. I have spoken at some length on the subject with the commander of the Falklands taskforce, and in his opinion, if we'd had a fixed wing carrier such as the *Ark Royal*, the whole operation could have been finished in ten days to 2 weeks, instead of the lengthy time it took. So, you are fortunate in having those and I sincerely hope, if we ever get into any operational situations again, we will be working side by side so that we can complement each other in these vital areas. (U.S.Navy)

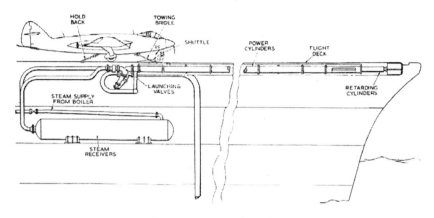

Steam catapult arrangement aboard a British carrier
Hawker Sea Hawk on the ramp

The Steam catapult arrangement

The United States Navy believed that the success of the steam catapult was due to the teamwork generated by Winkle Brown with the contractors, the scientists and the Royal Navy

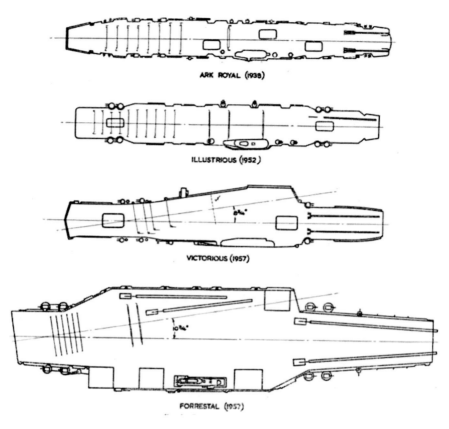

ARK ROYAL (1938)

ILLUSTRIOUS (1952)

VICTORIOUS (1957)

FORRESTAL (1957)

Carrier flight deck arrangements influenced by the steam catapult

HMS Argus, deck training aircraft carrier

HMS Audacity

HMS Avenger carrying two Swordfish

HMS Ravager

HMS Illustrious with Sea Fury, Avenger and Fireflies

HMS Indomitable deploying Sea Hurricanes, 1942

HMS Rocket

HMS Perseus, steam catapult trials ship

Cancelled CVA-01

Royal Navy Phantom FG1

Zero   *Heinkel Uhu*

He177 Greif

FW190

Junkers 88

Arado Blitz

Grumman Bearcat

Grumman Guardian

De Havilland Sea Vampire on HMS Ocean

Douglas Skyraider on HMS Perseus during catapult trials in 1952

HMS Perseus, trials vessel for the steam catapult

Gloster E28/39

Miles M20

Sea Hurricane

Fairey Barracuda

Grumman Avenger

Curtiss Helldiver

Messerschmitt Bf 109

Chance Vought Corsair.
On Brown's recommendation the Corsair was highly modified for Royal Navy
use. The wingtips were reduced in size, the undercarriage oleos adapted, tail
wheel lengthened and the cockpit modified. These modifications were carried
out by such aircraft manufacturers as Blackburn at Renfrew aerodrome.

Westland Wyvern, turboprop strike fighter

Brewster Buffalo

Blackburn Skua

De Havilland Sea Hornet

Bell P-39 Airacobra

Sea Mosquito

F-86 Sabre

Percival Pembroke

Miles M-35

Grumman Hellcat

Miles Martinet target tug

Grumman Cougar

Grumman Panther

Focke Wulf Condor

Hawker Tempest

Lancaster

Wellington

Handley Page Halifax

Avro Lincoln

Avro Tudor

Douglas Skymaster

Dakota IV

B-24 Liberator

Hoverfly on anti-submarine operations, MV Daghestan

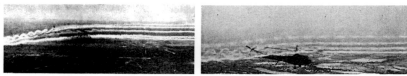

Hoverfly and Storch on smoke generated trials

Russian La7

Russian Il2

Fairey Fulmar aboard HMS Argus

Fairey Gannet

DeHavilland Sea Venom

Westand Wessex

Buccaneer S2

Scimitar

Sea Vixen

Martlet aboard
HMS Illustrious

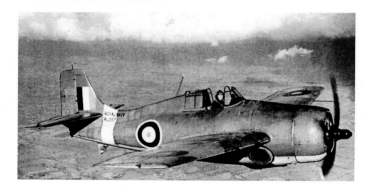

Grumman Martlet AL257, delivered to Scottish Aviation Prestwick
in August 1940 from the United States and seen over Maybole, Ayrshire.
Served with the Fleet Arm at Donibristle and Yeovilton